BEGINNING IN SIGHT

By the same author:

Non-fiction

A Voice in the Fire

BEGINNING IN SIGHT

THEODORE ELL

RECENT
WORK
PRESS

Beginning in Sight
Recent Work Press
Canberra, Australia

Copyright © Theodore Ell, 2022

ISBN: 9780645180862 (paperback)

A catalogue record for this
book is available from the
National Library of Australia

Cover image: *Ocean at Oregon Coast* by Nathalie Ross, 2013. Reproduced under Creative Commons attribution licence 2.0.
Cover design: Recent Work Press
Set by Recent Work Press

recentworkpress.com

ss

For Caitlin

Contents

4

Now. I would have you in, that would be a help,
but who knows how long the roads will still be clear—
so head home, I said, and give them all my love.

That was through the screen door. And the mesh was pressed
to the frame a bit as we talked—the first gusts
of a front—and then I might have raised the latch.

What stopped me was the new way we held our eyes,
our seeing right through, as the mesh went hard then slack.
For all that was said, we saw where we would be.

So, Head home, I said, and give them all my love.
For a while I watched the street, looked out for cars,
then closed up. On the porch, dry leaves flit in rings.

Too soon for dusk. Clouds that hide the sun still shift
and leave it. Shine left in the trees. Things might keep
in a fit state yet, though that makes for no news.

The lamps may not come on. What will come for us
is thought. We are young—it is the best of us,
the last friend to take its leave. Head home, I said,

and give them all my love

1

Mooring

for Robert Gray and Dee Jones

An estuary no road has reached. Staked mangrove flats,
forest shelved high above the sea-grass. On surfaces wavering and firm,
a brightness fit to crack. Beneath still keels,
green stirrings. Late lamplight in coves, where at some noons
white sails slide in or away. Slow skirmishing dragonflies.

Brief haven. Dwindling retreats. Vacant, intermittent houses
crouched over the shallows: slant timber, wavelets at doorsills.
Unfamiliar craft laying creels in the channels—
striped shoals hurry to gaps among the mudbanks
where the heron is poling. In stillness we suspect the present
   of outwitting us,

editing matters in our absence. The upriver wind
carries voices after every wake. If they too came
only in rare crossings, low hearsay,
as when thunder out to sea sends tremors through the ebb-tide pools—
then we might overhear the teeming that has weighed this air

past remembering, that drifts among the stilts of creaking floors. Know,
as though blind, an old touch at the elbow. Dive through
   the sun's clutches
from grey pier boards into cool cyphers.
Fluent silence, occlusion of echoes. Hours when not a vessel moves,
when the sky infiltrates standing water, screens cloud-abysses on the inlet—

then we might take peace unawares. Then hide it among these
   remnants, these appearances.

Molecules

for Beejay Silcox and Sam Allen

Storms have been holding off—wind-shy, turned away,
barred at the ranges—through multiplying summers.

Evenings still slip under an early shadow
that we recognise—there was no outrunning

the dinnertime hail, those drawn curtains of rain,
so we'd flatten and squeal into fuming soil

to throw thunderbolts off (that personal crash!)
then pick a way home through fields scoured pristine—

only now the great edge swells and barely moves,
the front of each reprise sheared off. Only spits

reach this far in, little taps on the shoulder
to turn and look: black stress over the forest,

nerve-gashes, many bow-waves pushing off rags
but never crossing to our cleared half-light.

The face of our days, bridling to change course,
a strop in the open that repels us home—

though now, as we head for roofs, is when some drops
may find old essence, bring it rising again,

alloying air hard: that scent, earthenware-warm,
of the readying soil, of storms it drank deep,

of want, enough stored to outlast a lifetime—
cloudbursts that have not passed the mind by, keep us

running, drenched and marked, in the path of lightning.

Grounding

for Laura Curotta

You lost your climbing trees—
the singing camphor-laurels
you would roam and memorise
like a hanging labyrinth,

all gangways, holding the world
in your private horizon days—
when the house and land were sold
and upbringing parcelled away.

Lean paths were laid. In far places
the future fretted every hour.
But your rehearsal was ageless—

your stepwise nerve, mind over wear,
to reach for tiered leaves of music—
to get a grip, then walk the air.

Cent

The scuttle of slim bronze under the tall counter—
that lost coin, fumbled from your pocket
like its minted glider from the nest-hole into airspace.

Cents taught ecology: two gliders equalled one parading frill-neck—
specimens now. And citizenship: Her Majesty
had a profile smaller than your fingernail.

Spotting a cent blinking up past your scuffed knees
made you smile like someone with a crush:
it would always buy a chocolate its own size.

The bellied jars of particoloured swirls
surely forecast silos full of justice.
That was before hunger. Life then was all

in small denominations. Nothing was zeroed.

Skimming

There are free

stones attractive to the palm
and I am

so often only what I do
if a half-tide

whiling over shingle
reveals a fit for the trigger-finger

that embeds there in the curl
the find will have me stand, turn

and farewell it
like a dart

so instant
the stone has made its tiptoe sprint

before I have imagined
where the traces end,

where the inscription fades.

Sundial

Restless August. Woolwich Road in the west wind:
a seam unsewn along the nape of the peninsula.

A sudden hot day. Fires far off. Stunned avenues
shed bark, turning an unscripted bronze

under smokescreen. From bare pavement eases tar.
Open ground is a soundless cry for a veranda.

Clouds are rising as a mangrove plumes above its rootlet city.

The border rivers lean together
in a trembling glaze, guesswork of sails.

Lanes, overhung. Their night emptiness. Only the glance
between the unlaced trees is wide awake.

Outspread limbs have started overlapping.
The cladding slips quietly from those amber shoulders.

Overhang

Wisteria flowers are all the tender words,
gazetted. It is not our turn to write them down.

The scented lanterns string along the veranda
as high above us the bright claims and rejoinders braid—

this grasping owner with its loose signature!
It has the dearest gems sewn up in colonies—

pavilions in leaflets—falling coinage patterning the boards
in soft chess. You watch it pocket the afternoon.

From budburst these flowers had a single cipher,
a choral dialect to drown out a dwelling pen.

The pleasures of this old house—they're only rented.

Ashore

A long fever, this afternoon. Sheet sun,
eyelid tremor, far roofs rippled as dunes,
pools hung amid rock and its likenesses,
horizons in your mind not fully closed.

Hours turn you over in shallows—the glass rim
between kelp scrapyards and capes,
mountainous rungs down a fraying ladder—
and the heat presses on, pushes time aside.

You are somewhere past the awning in the sky,
witnessing where everything is heading—
formations slide apart into the surf,
clouds roaring headway far inland—seeing

memories come undone, fish veins at gutting.

Freehold

Gale at Wollogorang. A barracking roar.

Footfalls taking the plain at a run from wall
to transparent wall. An ambush on daylight

mid-stride. Grass clutching after it overhead.
Ponds and reed-beds scissored apart. Pressed tree-lines

bent as flags: the prising of the grain. Glimpses
of rearrangement. As if a coverlet

lifted and shaken would model new hillsides.
As if an unstrung vine would throw a road off,

sling tar. Sheer weight mows sun into avenues,
battles to cull loose wood and stake new orchards,

a charge finding loopholes in the barricade
of settled shapes. As if to clear the homesteads,

take up the trodden floor, part land, peer in.

Heyday

You remember how the old home used to be.
Dry leaves matting the roof, loose doors, cobwebbed eaves.
Ready for doing up when we got round to it.

The fire-front took it like a hinge, back-broke it off.

To this day, there's only grass over brick-dust
and pitted cement. No sapling can go deep.
I don't hear many birds now or brush underfoot—

the new forest stands back in trained silences.

Chills, some mornings, and the scarp is still with me—
baked sandstone comes off like plates and pages now—
and I sometimes see slant shadows in the mist,

fixed bayonets. Warnings for the last to know.

As sunlight fills the chimney in the open
you see it holds our heyday, our beginnings
litter in the hearth. Spring has been torn from your years—

I nurse the next one, scattered, the soil my lifetime.

Disappearance

Newsprint and yellowed clippings
keep them forever children,

the frocked and tricycled siblings
smiling through decades that vanished.

Pictures from a certain era grow haloes in the end.

Nothing is left of the manhunts
or the wondering which remote road.

Now only a wasted young mother imagines
she knows the people in obituaries.

2

Generators

I

All patina, dial and pirouettes
the windmill

hovering above the corrugated roof
could be an airman,

standing, arms folded, by a runway,
knees locked in the gale streaming out his scarf,

admiring squadron after squadron
drumroll down to the lift frontier

and reach out in fading half-miles
all afternoon. The windmill,

so new to look at
you never knew which part to look at:

three-sided ladder, sunflower in chains,
face like a second's glare from a locomotive wheel,

slow cards dealing hand from hand
but not into a deck—

a sudden peak above the house
to take eyes off legwork one whole season

and keep McEnultys shaking their heads.
No bore, no pump or axles at its feet,

only the sight, from hills away,
of a stripling in shorts, all silhouettes

he climbed that quick about the scaffold,
wiring the heart of the fans

down a spindle in the middle,
or standing, sometimes, up top, watchful

it seemed, as though lightning could earth
there from a single slow wing of cloud.

Afternoons alone like that, up top.
(He had that way of frowning all through dinner,

piling up salt on his plate rim—
but then, he was off from the University—

no blame if he had thoughts tailing him.)
Then other crates came

on the Merriwa Flyer, the slowest train
in the Hunter, that never delivered firm ice cream,

and he was business all at once
in the shed he'd put up by the kitchen garden,

unpacking the deep black tubs
his diagrams called batteries

that he hooked up
to the cogged-in poles from up top

through just one crossways-spinning silver canister
and the wireless fanfared itself,

the verandas made a lantern of that hilltop
in nights no paraffin had travelled,

way was made for the Kelvinator
that would keep the cream cakes from running.

McEnultys electrified, and no wires out of Merriwa,
the talk of the backgammon boards

in the Fitzroy: Those relics powered up by some blow-in.
Say what you like about him, McEnultys said—

he paid his way for those term breaks,
that father of his not wanting the upkeep—

and went on to doctor bombers,
something to do with flying torpedoes, those swarms

the papers showed coming at battleships
out of gauze skies. He didn't give much away—

just kept earning more details for his epaulettes—
and squadrons would think little of him

stood out on the apron,
reading late cirrus, element-red

and corrugating over someone's hills,
propellers nearby idling down—though

there would be the windmill,
engineered, as McEnultys thought,

in his own image.

II

You'd swear it put whole acres
under glass—pasture in medleys, wheat parquet—

that microscope.
Every tick-over of a lens-piece

shows a map, an inlaid scene
in raw material.

Gridlock the colour of dry in a grass blade.
Channels and wells across red plains

in blood made flat under the coverslip,
the pin-end a looming pencil.

Nothing she won't trial,
jabbing her thumb

or picking up snakeskin
by the back step, to read dioramas

atlases only abridge.
Nor a minute missed

between finishing ice cream
(hard as teeth

but it will be years
till McEnultys have a gentler freezer)

and sitting up in the bureau chair
before bedtime, bowed to the eyepiece

as the eyepiece bows to the slide.
Sandalled feet past halfway to the floor.

Torchlight only, mostly cupped
in the mirror that fingers steer,

though the remainder
dimly includes her.

A smallholding at dusk
in a far region

of the long front room. Chills and loose wainscoting,
a night of the house's own.

Bedtime grows later
as McEnultys come to her, caller

by diffident caller,
knowing the hours but with a mind to let her be

(Let her, we ought to, they nod
over the china, her father might know aeroplanes

but there's nothing he'll do with her)
then stooping into the light, at her offer,

to gaze into a moth wing:
hairline creeks plotting shade for miles.

It's no dream she's looking into
but the maker's mark, McEnultys nod

into their chins. A pulse of rosary beads.
In these stays, handed on

from home, she's been used to seeing things dead—
that wether in the chute pen

coughing and pitched over
like it wanted to chafe its back off

and the rest trying to flee,
shuddered several thick at the rails,

a winded bag, legs rigid, all that's left
in the dirt ring—

though the microscope,
its fearful weight

newly handed down with ribbons and applause,
is telling of sources.

It's starting to seem there's company.
Dumb-useless, father calls that

before silence comes back into his face,
you go to Merriwa

till you grow a brain in your head.
It isn't him she'll think of

when she tilts the bottle and the calf drinks finally
that she's wrenched from deep inside

a stranded mother,
but grandsire McEnulty

in his threadbare crimson gown
taking up the doorway

and beckoning her quietly in again,
telling her, voice like flyscreen hinges,

never to get old—down the long front room:
dust-cloth, frost on windows,

lamplight on the little mauve and emerald panes
with their backs to the night air—

Never get old, girl.

III

A hole in brightness, a deletion
from dazed fields,

the shade inside an opened oil barrel
on a gate-pole:

a letterbox
not a word reaches,

just return airlifts
of the brown-papered doves

posting twigs into it
or inspecting the sky from the slot,

their cornerless hangar,
their apartment in the plains.

Cracked enamel, lichening rust,
wind in the dented aperture,

the name of McEnulty
in grey and separating wood

hung from pinched eye-hooks:
the letterbox,

the fixture
of cold morning vacancies

when lone tree-shadows
whiten the soil

and the parallel foot-trails
dotting acres of crystals

belong to the siblings,
meandering

through the sleep frontier
for small treasure

(have the tenants delivered
in the armoured nest

among the pale castoff-feathers?),
out from crumpled eaves,

a grey veranda.
There, walled in distance,

the living Miss McEnulty in her dark wool-cords
sighs into bent wicker,

blows steam off fogged tea, waits
as her other guest peels sheets

off trenched mattresses: the sleeve-rolled mother
of those two (who hardly need watching after

though it's a change
to see something moving in the mornings).

A girl for whom sprung midday grasses
are limbering a canter-stride,

a boy who from winter dawn air
is learning the feel of the razor—

a pair who think of grouped eggs
in one greater shell

as familiar and likely (never mind
their mother's harping on the breeding season,

those cells she insists on), who have a way of reckoning
the gist of cross-talk dinners

with glances
replying to glances,

who gather from frowned silence
that the chutes and gated aisles

of the shearers' labyrinth
where they can outrun barred sunlight

may be filled with little else
past these years,

who find a rosary in cracked mud in the dam
where it can only have been thrown—

who wonder how the old lady
beneath the gap-toothed motionless

windmill
could have been born at all,

looking like a mist
will walk off with her,

though what they're told
of when she was new

beneath that spun bullseye
tells them of all births at once.

A crossing in their personhood,
this one memory they can step inside.

Sun, again, as in a lens. Frost
dissolving as spilled salt.

Far up, a chalked line following
minute wingtips,

an arrow in blue silence.
Earthed, these peer selves

at the letterbox: their paired
whispers

turning in the barrel, eye
seeing forethoughts in eye,

then standing at intervals,
humming,

walking from time
to time,

their hill among hills.

Vessels

Albany, 1914

Lavish even for spring,
these brass mornings.
Picture-hats, flags and insignia,
anthems on the quay—

never mind the rust on the clear air,
milled and scuffed up
by four-abreast files
laddering the roads in khaki.

To anyone out near the ranges
there'd be only faint drumming
or bugle-heights, the odd training
shot, though on every road in

another sharp company's drilling
or chaffing over beef tins in tents
with tea from door-knock farms,
then propping slant rifles

down to the sea, a last street of stores
to the shoal of long steamers,
set jaws mulling towers of pipe-smoke.
Suddenly bound for a greater life,

they're putting aboard new-shaven grins
reared in towns like ours
that we won't ever visit but will think of,
often. This cargo is an age we've slept in.

In the spyglass, the surf round the low rocky spits
seems to nod to ship after dwindling ship—
raised arms above the handrails,
a man backed by sun high in rigging—

as they are ladled out on to the swell,
smoke trails at the glistening edge already.
Difficult. But they won't need pining
where they're going, or remember us long.

Sojourners

Sea-grass. Its endless stroke, that acquiescence
to a reigning swell, surely divined this cove

for the dozing pennants, the bared nodding masts
of quarantine. A landing in adjournment:

journey's end might come ashore with us. Quayside
and forest bluffs quaked at our first steps, turned us

flimsy as medicine in phials. Through starched days,
long passage. Rumours in whitewashed wards, inklings

of blood in caught breath, the sudden empty beds
where a propped head whispered only yesterday.

Solace for the sickened eye: birds in new paint,
unhurried tides, moonlight walking on the sea.

And daily for more among our berthed number
comes the leave-taking, the standstill of faces.

Those whom life turns against have never loved it
as now, with days to spend in it, in haven

with their small resisting cargo: one sleeper
woke his aisle with commands of sharp trim to sails,

and one man withered to clamshell hide spoke once
the whole anchorage, a prayer to the fine-robed

procession of guardians past the bright door—
we the revived, halting by veranda poles,

eyelids half-closed against hours that see through us,
uncertain of our weight. They have etched our names,

those enterprising crewmen, in yielding stone
that seams and shoulders storeys of the forest,

among carved lettering from before our time—
niche tablet manifests, familiar helm wheels,

spread albatross wings shielding an aged date—
years we relive, inmates of the same reprieve,

not to be parted till the gripping fingers
of thickening trees pull back the crevices,

cut loose the hulls of rock. Come embarking day
for the questioning few we have been honed to,

it is the cliffs we farewell, prelude headstones
we have been added to. We dare not yet cheer

nor can we wring one another's hands for long—
we are relearning strength with the tilt of decks,

as we recede as hopes from the headland rooms
where brisk heels tap their warnings past the re-made beds.

American misgivings

Pilgrimage

The Atlantic would insist. Every dawn
it overthrew rolled acres,

in dissonance viol-bowed our rigging.
Once it harrowed us ashore

the wailing kept us among dim coves and islets
where lank scowling herons revived the mystery-plays.

And vastly did we dream
of meadows in mastered sunlight,

vexed as we were by peoples on whose untilled earth
we had loosed our Atlantic tutelage—

and still seek we mercy for howling them under
to sow wind unto ourselves,

for we came of a great unending sermon
and weren't used to being interrupted.

Wood-trail

Taking a constitutional
round these parts in the Fall

with mellowing parchment overhead
and its scaffold of knitted quill-strokes—

that was rest, settling time, a braked inheritance,
until lately. The chill comes younger

at our throats, the leaves won't bide:
it lays hold and already they've loosened,

dollars slipping from a fortune
or a red loan, counties wide—a ceiling

brandished apart, sky seeing evermore through.
We find it's too far to hike now

through this dear bequest, on all behalves,
to find the evergreens.

Express

She'll steam no more. Better still,
exhibited. Don't let me steer you wrong:

it was crack firemanship,
the day-long sundown of coal-stoking—

we were a buffalo charge on tethered clouds, Tabernacle
organ pipes all going to glory,

us riding footplates through mountain sun
flickered like a shower in the firs—

but you feel for folks up sidings
that didn't go far, our echo over their farms,

us shedding flatirons and pan-handles
till their names stuck in the land—

it's like we sowed rust
and no wonder.

Moonshot

In our capsule
it's as if we're street kids

poking around in a Laundromat,
these keys and dials

everywhere at eye-level,
and us just hanging,

casing gaps between machines,
checking out the pipes and vents,

done with trying to peek
at what's turning in the murky portholes—

the memory's better,
of the find that got us in here:

rainfall glittering on the sidewalk by the door,
all around one dropped dime.

Turning circle

Always told he was not what school boards were looking for,
the buses took him on. An urban historian.
After all—the panel joked—he knew the streets backwards.
Like those coins turned up by workmen unearthing a mains,
he told himself, let history drip from the pay and then outgrow
the job. He had survived one interview. Cover meant plans.

But from the first day a bus heaved out under his hand
bookshelves filed away like the empty seats behind him.
He woke up to other kinds of time. Sources, unopened,
pooled around the bed, then met their due dates one by one.
The hours were numbered. His reading lens was a windscreen.
Contours and blank were drawn into routes, rostered and briefed.

Small hours would find the wheel already dished up to him,
a rim of travel corrugating his fingers.
Faces would step in from night to people his long room.
He learned the silence of early risers and latecomers.
Dawns in cloud were the best companions: the pale glimpses,
the snug chill, the westward grid a night sky that kept its stars.

Daylight was for talk—all overheard, after the fares:
the snapped business calls, old dears with memories,
young ones with nothing but the edge of their own voices.
Depot traffic bulletins never barked at him by name.
He heard that in the endless murmur of the map,
streets archiving his past in long lines, reciting the flats,

the lace bandstands, the dated school capstones, terrain covered in plans:
serenities and outbursts in the argument of homes,
surviving notes turned up from New Works Boards gone under.
A day of mind unharmed, he might climb the stairs still warm.
His building had no lift. Early riser and latecomer
there in his short room, his cleared bed of career. In dreams

he was a bright pause only, a citywide veneer.

3

Silhouettes

Mannequins, posed in the locked shopfront of an empty afternoon,

are Young Death's company, as he meanders the shaded rims
of silent squares. Young Death, the overtaker, strolls.
A student only, undoing all this sunlight is beyond his skill.
He leaves air-tremors idling and there is pleasure in the play
of brief shadows in the streets. He will not race them yet.

Around him is a brilliance so gentle only he can recognise it as the future.

When at last he meets a couple hand in hand cherishing their qualms
he stops until they look him in the eye. For this, he is trained:
in passing, they learn what darkness they are holding skin to skin.
Though it hurries them on to distressed sheets and a late calm
he need not watch them go: he has joined them, will sweat with them,

lead them behind glass, ageless as the hour. Peopling the arcades.

Verges

I

We're away: a carload of drift and sidekicks
opening up in empty districts, back roads
laying on a smelted hardening enamel

that we sneer over, throttle and sheet, skewered
for huge yelling moments then headlong again
inside speed, like we're slicing up sound to split

echoes and race them to creased hills between trees,
that whole interim to howl in—till we're peaked
on a crest corner that bends us throat-heaving

face-to the hind chevrons, blazed hornet-alarm,
of a truck's slogging dump tray, earth cuds tons high,
barring our dash—and heeling, we're pinion-swiped

in unison flail for the sidebar, grass aisle,
gavelled over white guide-posts—cliffs of quiet, breath
stayed—and dead ahead, red-eyed, the reflectors.

II

Not so elder, though there was old labour
in his heave and dip at the handlebars,
bowing to keep the pedals ticking over,

an abrupt back-into-it as we cruised nearer:
rear wheel laden side to side, all kit and gear,
the caricature of a snail swagger—

then in rear-vision, us craning for a gander:
unshaven dewlaps in a limp collar,
helmet aslant on loose fringes, chapped lips ajar,

and wavering left, back left, at each rightward tilt,
bowls that each car's aftermath blew him into
as further headlights passed him down the line,

his company Lake George's vacant floor,
mistletoes still glossy in trees they'd sapped spare—
sundowns in leaf, statesmanlike beards in mid-air.

III

A detour she asked for, a slower way home
via a house long parted with, her grandmother's,
down unlit avenues—into her mind's eye,

past dim lawns, bare trees wickering the late red—
lean veils glimpsed high over the mountains—detours
her source perhaps, now you are both not all that young,

of right of way, for keeping inroads open
while the drive lasts, for lengthening company—
though you feel the light voiding out of her talk

as she falls to reading only street numbers,
craning for remembered gestures in the kerb—
and where the house was, the warmth she won't describe:

hillside, your suburb glittering far away,
new wood ribs in the shape of eaves. Her quiet shrug.
The empty thoroughfares. There is no telling.

IV

Below the lamp, the pools. Dim asphalt scales,
glass slicks on tarmac. Cloud roofing parkland,
no thunder left. A roadside, a rim of the deep.

This last house-row, where your footfalls lead. Jetsam,
you are. Streets scheme you aside. Night is reprieve.
Thickets at windows: let darkness have its rooms,

its halls, let—underfoot *Crux!*... Below the lamp,
the snails. Down the lit path, a line vacating
yards for long grass, back-turned tenants mid-paving,

edging past the fallen vertebrae of a branch
as a flotilla bears round an outlying cape.
Skiffs and their shadows. Filled spinnakers, wake for miles:

an unmoved foiled sea, a bygone course holding.
The curb to pause upon, skirting blown wreckage—
drift to ease the passing, the moving over.

Whitsunday Passage

Where, wearing love's cast-offs and dreading all faces,
once ever, I wished not to be saved from poetry.

The shielding stance of the waves, ushering islands away.
Slender hands—blue veins beneath those shining robes—

leading émigré mountains, arms around their offspring,
towards the vanishing line, where broken spray glimmers

sometimes, beckons from past the edge. The rumoured
mazes of the reef. A distant laughter. Beside me, mute sands,

sleepless, altering their shapes. Drifting in the end and wading out.
For the disbanding of years. Its beginning in sight.

Alone

How small a word it takes to fill a whole night.

This swept-out house still has that seedling in it—
the tenant's trained, inevitable silence,
the front door like a turned back that has clamped to.

Footfalls outside are passing, not returning.

Half a bed is taken up with thoughts of touch,
ownership that multiplies like promises.
A creak echoes. All the shelves hold is moonlight.

An immense room, the uninhabited heart.

Window-seat

Dressed. Luggage in the hall.

Blank wainscoting,
hard little dents in carpet—
flooring, too wide to look at.

I try to go missing from the room,
between one minute and the next.
Sit in the window, with the mountains.

The winter noon
passes over the snowline. Dark rings
spread under the ridges.

Such surfaces—sights for amendment to travel across—

how they play at cancelling
the last moment!
Pretending this onward standstill

is no more than the drone
of the calendar's unsingable verses—
not the breath before the cry

when I am come for. When I will
long for this distance to adopt me. When I will pray,
with all my strength, to become again the child

who knew how to kill another hour.

Gossamer

With only daylight to go on
as if it were a fingertip homing on a map,
a silk tendril skimmed my neckline

and turned my head,
in time to hover out of reach
uncoiling a long insignia

right beneath the sun—
a ribbon vane,
a seam at the edge of anguish

where you'd believe
we can look close and never move—
until my eyelids came crashing down

like shutters in the bruise of wind
rifling the grassland,
playing the winnower,

sorting ends from odds
to pick more lines untied
and hurl chains of spun glass—

spindrift
off a cataract—
almost on me.

Tenebrae

Nightfall on the sill. Trinkets, hardened dust. Sky
in the gaps of a broken comb—the medley

of towers, antennae. The city: a queue
for dinner at a swish place, or a catwalk.

Thoughts of not doing an evening by halves—
not dress circles or crystal filled in series,

only forgetting the rule of doubt for hours,
leaving morning till morning, whole vacancies.

This sill, monogrammed by wine rims. A living.
Rest from studying the pavement in silent lines,

from the cold communion, aid. Frail-voiced
nuns chant responses from behind gilt fences

through the workless days. They reach some in the street,
who look in, down a ribcage of coloured light,

high rafters, canopy—a keyhole vision
of dusk between towers, that toothed horizon,

a light that breaks our outline, hides our numbers.

A yield

No cliffs, only a rounding off into the sea.
The pasture slopes and just gives way.
There is this shape along the inlet
where breakers shy from digging at the edge,
though some days they turn.

When I am down there, do not come looking for me.
It is exposed. There is a blame of wind.
And if the turf goes, there is no hitching you back
up from that hem.
For a moment you will have silver waves below your feet,
then it will be all cold noise and traffic.
You are on the verges of a great highway there.

It is where I find myself on the long days of a good season.
You will know them
because I will refuse to come up home
even when you call out the time.
I will be out of earshot, thinking,

Those are the millimetres I must plough.

4

Sun-shower

Late in the year, a lifted blind

let in reunions. Light beating on the leaves.
A likeness had come over the days

to forerunners peopled with smaller shadows,

as though old friends were coming home
to bargain for extensions on the past,

make disclosures from before
the crowding-out of life. Hesitant warmth

in light of words that left their handprints on the mirror.

Pressure to tread lightly
on the grass spears, barefoot even:

there was recovery in the turf
though a sole could best what the drought had not.

Then the clouds, encountering errors, thinned away.

Not the peace we were preparing for—
though perhaps a truce with silence.

A noon for me, a keepsake.

Watershed

for Caitlin

Sleep over ministering sleep,
tresses of rain

drift over the lake—
pins and needles,

intermittent silvers
where no depths stir:

water rising to know water,
allaying creases.

At last this is your only pain,
these roaming films.

Before you entered the eclipse
you harboured scalding resin,

a cloyed frieze
that has been lifted clear.

Mountain-pillowed,
evened, you will show

the lasting graces
of the freshly spared.

Votive lines

in memory of Dahlia Martin

I

Friend, you have left hours of silence,

conversations where you alone knew what to say—
and now you have gone where only poems can follow

you have become everything our talk dared to conjecture

—and I am no more than an exam being handed in,
paper, quaking and teeming

with what you have asked of me.

II

With mists over vacant playing fields

and mountains half-hidden in the poplar-rows
conspiring about ice,

those mornings put spring off and off again
and slid their canopy over the lawns and skylights

(a little sunlight giving it the slip,
making for long paths, clearings)—

until everywhere had the one ceiling
that lowered the hills,

trailed cobwebs of rain,
tamped the land down to a too-furnished room

haunted by slips and collisions
and where an hour is a memory of an hour—

save that one oversight,
a fault in the grey bargaining

when the bars of a downpour parted, showing other heights,
and the black plating of the streets kindled up small clouds of its own,

offered the deluge back.

III

When there was no language left in the air,
winds without breath,

waves came sliding towards the lake-edge—

inked reminders pushed under a closed door,
sheet after prompting sheet.

Floodplain

I

Spring rain, far from now. Old waters sleep in fens
where they rose once over fields. Trees must wade still.

Where driftwood settles, fences kneel. Holed brick walls
stencil the sky's rims on each wave.

II

A barge, pushed head-down in the mire. Hull opened
by vanished torrents, ribs pried out. Grey gunwales

soaked and mossed—the sun here keeps uncertain hours.
An island taking root, hemmed with staves of reeds,

lips of shell. A lone bittern tails shy quarry
in wheelhouse and companionway.

III

The grip of hidden clay, pulling ever down—
red iron knuckles clasping on worn timber—

the separate circles of levelling rain—
brimmings of incomplete events.

Hereafter

Sunrise hesitated. Where glass panes faced east
they caught a gilt stare that outlived an instant,

made birds break off their chat on new sprigs and look,
slowed breeze that chafed bark, creaking as the cane chairs

in which we sat—and where sunrise found us, up
and watching for it. Errors uncorrected,

the first so far on the meticulous scroll
this day was inscribing over the rough ground

of the last. With first light hanging, our cups steamed.
We may have known then what it is to be ghosts,

but that was nothing. The sheer dead stop, the red face
of the sun—that was our delight: to have dazed

the morning, vexed it, forced it to hold its nerve!

Convalescence

Walking unaided now, he can tend the garden.
While he was gone the creepers folded out tendrils
enough to fill in many days with clearing ground.
Clip by clip the turf is uncovered to the sun.

He strolls the new borders, thin under his hat brim.

Spying out shoots, he mingles among training poles
and winds a few wild stems gently along guidelines.
When he can lift, he will patch the cladding of the porch;
light has worn through. He strokes the ripples in the iron.

His frail tread firms on cushioned and clean-shaven lawn.

There are waking designs that were never with him.
He thinks of beds, makes plans to make paths around them,
with his own hands lays the first bricks. With his own hands.
Fitting the gloves of their own selves. It never ends,

the thought that he nearly slimmed out of reach of time.

Notes

'Heyday': 'Spring has been torn from your years'—see Herodotus, *Histories*, VII: 8.

Acknowledgements

I thank my wife, Caitlin Bell, for her loving support, through everything.

I am immensely grateful to Shane Strange and Recent Work Press for believing in this book. I also warmly thank Martin Dolan for his perceptive reading of the manuscript.

Certain friends have helped to shape this book over many years with advice and encouragement. In particular I wish to thank Robert Gray, Beejay Silcox, Jamie Grant, Elias Greig, Alexandra Hankinson, Mark O'Connor, Sarah Kennedy, Melinda Smith, Paolo Totaro, Vincent Moleta, Erin Martine Sessions, Chris Oakey, Keri Rehfisch, Melissa Macomber, Luke Whitington and Matthew Asprey Gear. My loving thanks also go to my parents, Jonathan and Suzanne, and to the Nussey, Nottidge, Garsed and Bell families.

I thank Kim Fasher and Sarah Mosca for the opportunity to contribute to the *Life is Hard* exhibition catalogue at Firstdraft Gallery in 2014, which set this book on its course, though I did not know it then.

I thank my colleagues at the Australian National University, particularly Katie Sutton, Catherine Travis, Ros Smith, Gemma King and Leslie Barnes, for their support and for the opportunities that the School of Literature, Languages and Linguistics has afforded me.

Lastly, I thank the editors of publications in which some of these poems have appeared previously: Michael Schmidt, John McAuliffe, Peter Rose, James Jiang, Jaya Savige, Susan Wyndham, Mark Tredinnick, Alice Ford, Jean Kent, David Musgrave, Carolyn Rickett, Jen Webb and Rima Rantisi.

'Tenebrae,' *Australian Book Review* 442 (May 2022), p. 41.

'A yield' and 'Generators—I, II, III,' *PN Review* 261 (2021), pp. 42-45.

'Sun-shower,' *The Australian*, 'Review,' 31 July 2021, p. 18 and *This Gift, This Poem*, ed. Kent, Musgrave et al (Waratah, NSW: Puncher & Wattmann, 2021), pp. 54-55.

'Verges (I),' *The Australian*, 'Review,' 9-10 January 2021, p. 17.

'Freehold,' *The Australian*, 'Review,' 17 October 2020, p. 17.

'Ashore,' *Rusted Radishes* 8 (Beirut: American University of Beirut, 2020), p. 96.

'Overhang,' *The Australian*, 'Review,' 17 November 2018, p. 18.

'Verges (II),' *The Canberra Times*, 'Panorama,' 26 August 2017, p. 17.

'Moonshot' from 'American Misgivings,' *The Canberra Times*, 'Panorama,' 2-3 July 2016, p. 18.

'Sundial,' *The Australian*, 'Review,' 28-29 November 2015, p. 20.

'Grounding,' *The Australian*, 'Review,' 1-2 August 2015, p. 19.

'A yield,' in an earlier prose form as part of a suite called 'Half-glasses,' *Life is Hard: Exhibition Catalogue* (Sydney: Firstdraft Gallery, 2014, ed. Natalya Hughes and Todd McMillan).

'Alone,' *Australian Love Poems 2013* (Melbourne: Inkerman and Blunt, 2013, ed. Mark Tredinnick), p. 286.

'Turning circle,' *Cuttings, Issue 1: In Real Life* (August 2013). E-magazine.

'Cent,' *Cuttings, Issue 0: A Cosy Catastrophe* (February 2013). E-magazine.

'Convalescence,' *Sydney Morning Herald*, 'Spectrum', 12-13 May 2012, p. 39.

'Disappearance,' *Sydney Morning Herald*, 'Spectrum', 19-20 March 2011, p. 35.

About the Author

Theodore Ell was born in Sydney in 1984. He studied literature and modern languages at the University of Sydney, spent time in Bologna and Florence for research, and was awarded a PhD in 2010. For several years he worked freelance as an editor, translator and researcher, work that culminated in his book *A Voice in the Fire*, which brought to light unknown Italian anti-fascist writing. During this time, he also co-founded the international journal *Contrappasso Magazine*, of which he was co-editor for four years. In 2013, he edited the anthology *Long Glances* for Manning Clark House in Canberra. He moved to Canberra in 2015 to begin working in the public service. In 2018, he accompanied his wife on a diplomatic posting to Lebanon, and while living in Beirut, they survived the port explosion of August 2020, which destroyed their home. Returning to Australia in early 2021, they settled in Canberra once again.

Theodore's poetry, essays, translations and non-fiction have been published in Australia, Italy, the UK and Lebanon. His essay 'Façades of Lebanon,' about that country's year of revolution and the experience of the explosion, won the 2021 Calibre Essay Prize. He is an honorary lecturer in literature at the Australian National University.